Ruby Tuesday
Readers

Mole

By Ruth Owen

Reading Consultant:
Beth Walker Gambro

Published in 2018 by Ruby Tuesday Books Ltd.

Copyright © 2018 Ruby Tuesday Books Ltd.

Designer: Emma Randall
Production: John Lingham

Photo Credits:
Alamy: Cover, 1, 6, 11, 12, 23 (bottom); Biosphoto: 19, 22 (top); Getty Images: 14–15, 17, 22 (bottom); Shutterstock: 3, 4, 5, 9, 13, 16, 20, 21, 22 (center), 23 (top), 24.

Library of Congress Control Number: 2018906345
Print (hardback) ISBN 978-1-78856-060-3
Print (paperback) ISBN 978-1-78856-073-3
eBook ISBN 978-1-78856-061-0

Printed and published in the United States of America.

For further information including rights and permissions requests, please contact our Customer Services Department at 877-337-8577.

Contents

What happened last night?

There are small piles of
soil all over the grass.

molehill

They are **molehills**!

Last night a tiny mole was digging tunnels under the ground.

mole

large feet

A mole is about 6 inches (15 cm) long.

Now the mole is digging another tunnel.

She digs with her front feet and sharp claws.

tunnel

The tunnel is soon filled with lots of loose soil.

The mole digs a tunnel up to the surface.

Then she pushes the loose soil out of the tunnel onto the grass and makes . . .

. . . another molehill!

The mole digs about 65 feet (20 m) of tunnels a day.

She also digs rooms called **chambers**, where she sleeps.

molehill

chamber

tunnels

The mole cannot see very well, but she uses her whiskers to feel **vibrations**.

Suddenly, the mole feels some vibrations under the ground.

She runs along a tunnel and finds a fat worm.

Yum!

Worms are the mole's favorite food.

She eats about 20 worms a day.

Sometimes she eats baby insects, called **larvae**.

a larva, or caterpillar

One day the mole feels vibrations under the ground.

A male mole is digging into her tunnel.

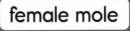

female mole

The male wants to **mate** with her.

male mole

After mating, the male mole goes back to his own tunnel.

Now the female mole digs a special chamber.

She climbs out of a molehill and gets grass to make a soft bed.

About 28 days after mating, the mole gives birth to four babies in the chamber.

baby mole

The tiny babies have no fur, and they cannot see.

The baby moles drink milk from their mother's body.

Soon, sharp claws for digging grow from their feet.

At seven weeks old, they can dig tunnels and find worms.

Now they must leave their mother and dig their own homes.

a five-week-old mole

The young moles climb out of their mother's home.

They are not safe.

Foxes, owls, and cats may try to eat them.

The little moles quickly dig their own safe homes.

Mother mole is busy digging for worms!

Glossary

chamber (CHAYM-bur)
A room or a space that has walls, a ceiling, and a floor.

larva (LAR-vuh)
A young animal. The larvae of insects usually have long, fat bodies.

mate (MATE)
To get together to produce young.

molehill (MOHL-hil)
A small heap of crumbly soil that a mole has pushed up to the surface from its tunnel.

vibrations (vye-BRAY-shunz)
Shaking movements back and forth or from side to side.

Index

Read More

Rake, Jody S. *Meerkats, Moles, and Voles: Animals of the Underground (First Facts)*. North Mankato, MN: Capstone Press (2016).

Sebastian, Emily & Julio Gil. *Moles (Animals Underground)*. New York: Rosen Publishing (2012).

Learn More Online

To learn more about moles, go to:
www.rubytuesdaybooks.com/wildlifewatchers